Nativity

Celebrate the real reason behind the season.
With these 8 crochet figures you can decorate your home and tell the story of the birth of Jesus.

LEISURE ARTS, INC.
Maumelle, Arkansas

Contents

Meet Kristi Simpson

Inspired by her love of yarn, Kristi Simpson creates crochet, knit, and macramé projects with a fresh and modern touch. The mother of five became hooked on crochet after teaching herself so she could teach her daughter to make a scarf from a learn-to-crochet kit that was a gift.

"I loved it from the beginning," she says, "I'm amazed that I could take a strand of yarn and create something so useful and pretty! Needless to say, I never stopped."

Kristi loves all crafts, including cardmaking and scrapbooking.

Look for other Leisure Arts books featuring Kristi's designs at https://leisurearts.com/kristi-simpson/.

Holy Family

EASY

SHOPPING LIST

Yarn (Medium Weight)

MEDIUM 4

- ☐ Brown - 36 yards (33 meters)
- ☐ Cream - 35 yards (32 meters)
- ☐ Lt Blue - 35 yards (32 meters)
- ☐ Tan - 18 yards (16.5 meters)
- ☐ Lt Brown - 12 yards (11 meters)
- ☐ Dk Blue - 12 yards (11 meters)
- ☐ Yellow - 10 yards (9 meters)

Crochet Hook

- ☐ Size D (3.25 mm) **or** size needed for gauge

Additional Supplies

- ☐ Yarn needle
- ☐ Polyester fiberfill

STITCH GUIDE

INVISIBLE SINGLE CROCHET 2 TOGETHER

(abbreviated invisible sc2tog)

Pull up a loop in Front Loop Only of each of next 2 sts ***(Fig. 2, page 47)***, YO and draw through all 3 loops on hook **(counts as one sc)**.

JOSEPH

Finished Size: 5¾" (14.5 cm) tall

Gauge Information

Gauge Swatch: 2" (5 cm) diameter

Work same as Base: 30 sts.

Base

Rnd 1 (Right side): With Brown, make an adjustable ring and work 6 sc in ring ***(Figs. 1a-d, page 46)***; do **not** join, place marker to indicate the beginning of the rnd ***(see Markers, page 45)***.

Note: Loop a short piece of yarn around any stitch to mark Rnd 1 as **right** side.

Rnd 2: 2 Sc in each sc around: 12 sc.

Rnd 3: (Sc in next sc, 2 sc in next sc) around: 18 sc.

Rnd 4: (Sc in next 2 sc, 2 sc in next sc) around: 24 sc.

Rnd 5: (Sc in next 3 sc, 2 sc in next sc) around; slip st in next sc, do **not** finish off: 30 sts.

Body

Rnd 6: Ch 1, sc in Back Loop Only of same st as slip st and each sc around ***(Fig. 2, page 47)***; join with slip st to **both** loops of first sc: 30 sc.

Rnd 7: Ch 1, sc in same st as joining and in each sc around; do **not** join, place marker to indicate the beginning of the rnd.

Rnds 8 and 9: Sc in each sc around; at end of Rnd 9, slip st in next sc and finish off.

Rnd 10: With **right** side facing, join Cream with sc in same st as slip st ***(see Joining With Sc, page 45)***; sc in each sc around; join with slip st to first sc.

Rnd 11: Ch 1, sc in same st as joining and in each sc around; do **not** join, place marker to indicate the beginning of the rnd.

Rnds 12-14: Sc in each sc around.

Rnds 15 and 16: Invisible sc2tog, sc in each sc around: 28 sc.

Rnd 17: (Sc in next 5 sc, invisible sc2tog) around: 24 sc.

Rnds 18 and 19: Sc in each sc around.

Rnd 20: (Sc in next 4 sc, invisible sc2tog) around: 20 sc.

Rnds 21 and 22: Sc in each sc around.

Rnd 23: (Sc in next 3 sc, invisible sc2tog) around: 16 sc.

Rnd 24: Sc in each sc around.

Stuff Body with polyester fiberfill.

Rnd 25: (Sc in next 2 sc, invisible sc2tog) around: 12 sc.

Rnd 26: (Sc in next sc, invisible sc2tog) around; slip st in next sc and finish off: 8 sts.

Head

Rnd 27: With **right** side facing, join Tan with sc in same st as slip st; sc in same st, 2 sc in each sc around; join with slip st to first sc: 16 sc.

Rnd 28: Ch 1, sc in same st as joining and in next 2 sc, 2 sc in next sc, (sc in next 3 sc, 2 sc in next sc) around; do **not** join, place marker to indicate the beginning of the rnd: 20 sc.

Rnds 29-31: Sc in each sc around.

Rnd 32: (Sc in next 3 sc, invisible sc2tog) around: 16 sc.

Stuff Head with polyester fiberfill.

Rnd 33: (Sc in next 2 sc, invisible sc2tog) around: 12 sc.

Rnd 34: (Sc in next sc, invisible sc2tog) around; slip st in next sc and finish off leaving a 6" (15 cm) end for sewing: 8 sts.

Thread yarn needle with end and weave yarn through Front Loop Only of remaining sc; pull tightly to close and secure end.

Arm (Make 2)

With Cream, leaving a 6" (15 cm) end for sewing and beginning at wrist, ch 7; join with slip st to first ch to form a ring.

Rnd 1 (Right side): Ch 1, 7 sc in ring; do **not** join, place marker to indicate the beginning of the rnd.

Note: Mark Rnd 1 as **right** side.

Rnds 2-7: Sc in each sc around.

Rnd 8: Invisible sc2tog, sc in next 5 sc: 6 sc.

Rnds 9-11: Sc in each sc around; at end of Rnd 11, slip st in next sc and finish off leaving an 8" (20.5 cm) end for sewing.

HAND

Rnd 1 (Right side): With Tan, make an adjustable ring, ch 3, 3 dc in ring; join with slip st to top of beginning ch-3 and finish off.

Thread yarn needle with beginning end of Arm. Insert Hand into beginning ring of Arm and sew in place.

Headdress

Rnd 1 (Right side): With Lt Brown, make an adjustable ring and work 6 sc in ring; do **not** join, place marker to indicate the beginning of the rnd.

Note: Mark Rnd 1 as **right** side.

Rnd 2: 2 Sc in each sc around: 12 sc.

Rnd 3: (Sc in next sc, 2 sc in next sc) around: 18 sc.

Rnd 4: (Sc in next 8 sc, 2 sc in next sc) twice: 20 sc.

Rnd 5: Sc in Front Loop Only of each sc around; place marker in free loop **behind** last sc made for Hair placement ***(Fig. 3, page 47)***.

Rnd 6: Sc in both loops of each sc around; do **not** finish off.

FLAP

Row 1 (Wrong side): Ch 1, **turn**; sc in first 14 sc, leave remaining 6 sc unworked.

Rows 2-6: Ch 1, turn; sc in each sc across.

Finish off.

HAIR

Row 1: Holding **right** side of top of Headdress toward you and working in free loops on Rnd 4, join Brown with sc in marked loop; dc in next 7 free loops, sc in next free loop; do **not** finish off: 9 sts.

BEARD

Row 1: Ch 8, turn; skip first 8 sts, slip st in last sc: one ch-8 sp.

Row 2 (Right side)**:** Ch 1, turn; (2 sc, hdc, 3 dc, hdc, 2 sc) in ch-8 sp; slip st in last sc on Row 1 of Hair and finish off.

Note: Mark Row 2 as **right** side.

Sash

Row 1 (Right side)**:** With Lt Brown, ch 45; sc in second ch from hook and in each ch across: 44 sc.

Note: Mark Row 1 as **right** side.

Row 2: Ch 1, turn; slip st in Back Loop Only of each sc across; finish off.

Finishing

Using Photos as a guide for placement and using long ends:

- Sew Arms to Body.
- Placing center of Sash under left arm and crossing ends at right shoulder, tack Sash in place. Tack ends of Sash to Body.
- With Lt Brown, sew Headdress to Head

Mary

Finished Size: 5½" (14 cm) tall

Gauge Information

Gauge Swatch: 2" (5 cm) diameter
Work same as Base: 30 sts.

Base

Rnd 1 (Right side)**:** With Dk Blue, make an adjustable ring and work 6 sc in ring ***(Figs. 1a-d, page 46)***; do **not** join, place marker to indicate the beginning of the rnd ***(see Markers, page 45)***.

Note: Loop a short piece of yarn around any stitch to mark Rnd 1 as **right** side.

Rnd 2: 2 Sc in each sc around: 12 sc.

Rnd 3: (Sc in next sc, 2 sc in next sc) around: 18 sc.

Rnd 4: (Sc in next 2 sc, 2 sc in next sc) around: 24 sc.

Rnd 5: (Sc in next 3 sc, 2 sc in next sc) around; slip st in next sc, do **not** finish off: 30 sts.

Body

Rnd 6: Ch 1, sc in Back Loop Only of same st as slip st and each sc around ***(Fig. 2, page 47)***; join with slip st to **both** loops of first sc: 30 sc.

Rnd 7: Ch 1, sc in same st as joining and in each sc around; do **not** join, place marker to indicate the beginning of the rnd.

Rnd 8: Sc in each sc around; slip st in next sc and finish off.

Rnd 9: With **right** side facing, join Lt Blue with sc in same st as slip st ***(see Joining With Sc, page 45)***; sc in each sc around; join with slip st to first sc.

Rnd 10: Ch 1, sc in same st as joining and in each sc around; do **not** join, place marker to indicate the beginning of the rnd.

Rnds 11 and 12: Sc in each sc around.

Rnds 13 and 14: Invisible sc2tog, sc in each sc around: 28 sc.

Rnd 15: (Sc in next 5 sc, invisible sc2tog) around: 24 sc.

Rnd 16: Sc in each sc around.

Rnd 17: (Sc in next 4 sc, invisible sc2tog) around: 20 sc.

Rnds 18 and 19: Sc in each sc around.

Rnd 20: (Sc in next 3 sc, invisible sc2tog) around: 16 sc.

Rnd 21: Sc in each sc around.

Stuff Body with polyester fiberfill.

Rnd 22: (Sc in next 2 sc, invisible sc2tog) around: 12 sc.

Rnd 23: (Sc in next sc, invisible sc2tog) around; slip st in next sc and finish off: 8 sts.

Head

Rnd 24: With **right** side facing, join Tan with sc in same st as slip st; sc in same st, 2 sc in each sc around; join with slip st to first sc: 16 sc.

Rnd 25: Ch 1, sc in same st as joining and in next 2 sc, 2 sc in next sc, (sc in next 3 sc, 2 sc in next sc) around; do **not** join, place marker to indicate the beginning of the rnd: 20 sc.

Rnds 26-28: Sc in each sc around.

Rnd 29: (Sc in next 3 sc, invisible sc2tog) around: 16 sc.

Stuff Head with polyester fiberfill.

Rnd 30: (Sc in next 2 sc, invisible sc2tog) around: 12 sc.

Rnd 31: (Sc in next sc, invisible sc2tog) around; slip st in next sc and finish off leaving a 6" (15 cm) end for sewing: 8 sts.

Thread yarn needle with end and weave yarn through Front Loop Only of remaining sc; pull tightly to close and secure end.

Arm (Make 2)

With Lt Blue, leaving a 6" (15 cm) end for sewing and beginning at wrist, ch 7; join with slip st to first ch to form a ring.

Rnd 1 (Right side): Ch 1, 7 sc in ring; do **not** join, place marker to indicate the beginning of the rnd.

Rnds 2-7: Sc in each sc around.

Rnd 8: Invisible sc2tog, sc in next 5 sc: 6 sc.

Rnds 9 and 10: Sc in each sc around; at end of Rnd 10, slip st in next sc and finish off leaving an 8" (20.5 cm) end for sewing.

HAND

Rnd 1 (Right side): With Tan, make an adjustable ring, ch 3, 3 dc in ring; join with slip st to top of beginning ch-3 and finish off.

Thread yarn needle with beginning end of Arm. Insert Hand into beginning ring of Arm and sew in place.

Headdress

Rnd 1 (Right side): With Lt Blue, make an adjustable ring and work 6 sc in ring; do **not** join, place marker to indicate the beginning of the rnd.

Note: Mark Rnd 1 as **right** side.

Rnd 2: 2 Sc in each sc around: 12 sc.

Rnd 3: (Sc in next sc, 2 sc in next sc) around: 18 sc.

Rnd 4: (2 Sc in next sc, sc in next 8 sc) twice: 20 sc.

Rnd 5: (2 Sc in next sc, sc in next 9 sc) twice: 22 sc.

Rnd 6: Sc in each sc around.

Rnd 7: (Sc in next 9 sc, invisible sc2tog) twice; do **not** finish off: 20 sc.

FLAP

Row 1 (Wrong side): Ch 1, **turn**; sc in first 15 sc, leave remaining 5 sc unworked.

Rows 2-13: Ch 1, turn; sc in each sc across.

Finish off.

Trim: With **right** side facing, join Dk Blue with sc in the first sc on Row 13; sc in same st and in next 13 sc, 3 sc in last sc; sc evenly across ends of rows; sc in unworked sc on Rnd 7; sc evenly across ends of rows and in same sc as first sc; join with slip st to first sc, finish off.

HAIR

Part: With Brown, ch 5; finish off.

Cut sixteen 8" (20.5 cm) strands of Brown.

For each chain, hold 2 strands together and fold in half. Use crochet hook to draw fold through one side of chain, forming a loop. Pull ends of fringe through this loop. Pull to tighten. Make 4 fringes along each side of chain.

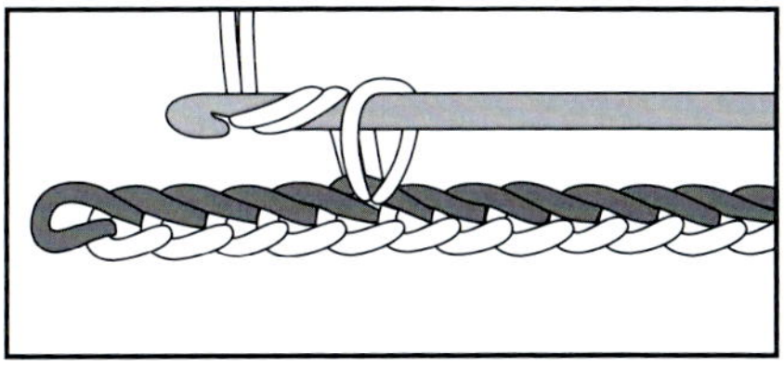

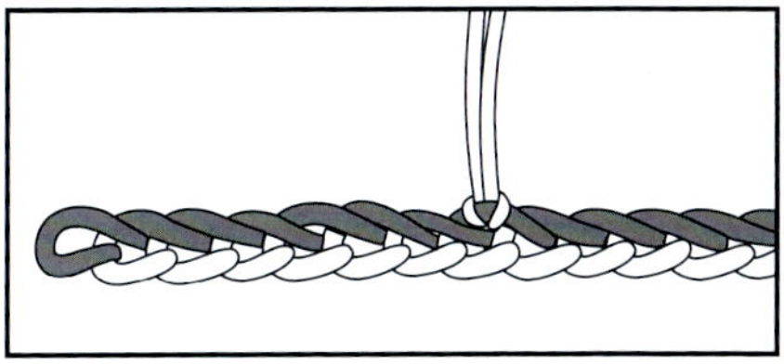

Pull hair to back base of head, neatly framing the face; wrap tightly, secure and finish off.
Trim Hair 1" (2.5 cm) below wrap.

Note: Hair does not have to be neat at top of the head or cover the back of the Head. It will be covered with Headdress. Framing the face is the main objective.

Finishing

Using Photos as a guide for placement and using long ends:

- Sew Arms to Body.
- With Lt Blue, sew Headdress to Head.

Baby Jesus

Finished Size: 3" wide x 1½" tall
(7.5 cm x 4 cm)

Gauge Information

22 sc and 20 rows/rounds = 4" (10 cm)

Gauge Swatch: 4" (10 cm) square

Ch 23.

Row 1: Sc in second ch from hook and in each ch across: 22 sc.

Rows 2-20: Ch 1, turn; sc in each sc across.

Finish off.

Head

Rnd 1 (Right side)**:** With Tan, make an adjustable ring and work 6 sc in ring ***(Figs. 1a-d, page 46)***; do **not** join, place marker to indicate the beginning of the rnd ***(see Markers, page 45)***.

Note: Loop a short piece of yarn around any stitch to mark Rnd 1 as **right** side.

Rnd 2: 2 Sc in each sc around: 12 sc.

Rnds 3 and 4: Sc in each sc around.

Stuff Head with polyester fiberfill.

Rnd 5: Invisible sc2tog 6 times; slip st in next sc and finish off leaving a 6" (15 cm) end for sewing: 6 sts.

Body

Rnd 6: With **right** side facing, join Lt Blue with sc in same st as slip st ***(see Joining With Sc, page 45)***; sc in same st, 2 sc in each sc around; join with slip st to first sc: 12 sc.

Rnd 7: Ch 1, sc in same st as joining and in each sc around; do **not** join, place marker to indicate the beginning of the rnd.

Rnds 8 and 9: Sc in each sc around.

Stuff Body with polyester fiberfill.

Rnd 10: Invisible sc2tog 6 times; slip st in next sc and finish off leaving a long end for sewing: 6 sts.

Thread yarn needle with end and weave yarn through Front Loop Only of remaining sc *(**Fig. 2, page 47**)*; pull tightly to close and secure end.

Wrap

With Cream, ch 26.

Row 1: Sc in second ch from hook and in each ch across: 25 sc.

Rows 2-4: Ch 1, turn; sc in each sc across.

Finish off leaving an 8" (20.5 cm) end for sewing.

Holding end of rows at the base of the Body, pull the Wrap over the top of the Head and back over the first end of the Wrap. Sew in place at feet. The back will remain open, but will not be seen when placed in the Manger.

Manger

With Brown, ch 30; being careful **not** to twist ch, join with slip st to first ch to form a ring.

Rnd 1 (Right side): Ch 1, sc in same ch as joining and each ch around; join with slip st to first sc: 30 sc.

Note: Mark Rnd 1 as **right** side.

Rnd 2: Ch 1, sc in same st as joining and in each sc around; do **not** join, place marker to indicate the beginning of the rnd.

Rnds 3 and 4: Sc in each sc around.

Rnd 5: ★ Sc in next 7 sc, invisible sc2tog, (sc in next sc, invisible sc2tog) twice; repeat from ★ once **more**: 24 sc.

Rnd 6: ★ Sc in next 6 sc, invisible sc2tog 3 times; repeat from ★ once **more**; slip st in next sc and finish off leaving an 8" (20.5 cm) end for sewing: 18 sts.

Thread yarn needle with end. Folding Rnd 6 of Manger in half and having the decreases at each end, sew Rnd 6 together through the **outside** loops only. The inside loops will be used to attach Yellow like fringe to represent Hay.

HAY

Cut fifty-four 6" (15 cm) strands of Yellow.
For each exposed loop (18) at bottom of Manger, hold 3 strands together and fold in half. Use crochet hook to draw fold through one side of st, forming a loop. Pull ends of yarn through this loop; pull to tighten.

Finishing

Lay Baby Jesus in the Manger in the center of the Hay. Thread yarn needle with Lt Blue and sew to Manger to secure.

Trim Hay evenly around Manger so that it is approximately ½" (12 mm) above the edge.

Angel

EASY

Finished Size: 5¼" (13.5 cm) tall

SHOPPING LIST

Yarn (Medium Weight) MEDIUM 4

- ☐ Cream - 41 yards (37.5 meters)
- ☐ Tan - 6 yards (5.5 meters)
- ☐ Yellow - 6 yards (5.5 meters)

Crochet Hook

- ☐ Size D (3.25 mm) **or** size needed for gauge

Additional Supplies

- ☐ Yarn needle
- ☐ Polyester fiberfill

Gauge Information

Gauge Swatch: 2" (5 cm) diameter

Work same as Base, page 20: 30 sts.

STITCH GUIDE

INVISIBLE SINGLE CROCHET 2 TOGETHER *(abbreviated invisible sc2tog)*
Pull up a loop in Front Loop Only of each of next 2 sts *(Fig. 2, page 47)*, YO and draw through all 3 loops on hook **(counts as one sc)**.

BEGINNING CLUSTER (uses one st)
Ch 2, ★ YO, insert hook in st indicated, YO and pull up a loop, YO and draw through 2 loops on hook; repeat from ★ once **more**, YO and draw through all 3 loops on hook.

CLUSTER (uses one sc)
★ YO, insert hook in sc indicated, YO and pull up a loop, YO and draw through 2 loops on hook; repeat from ★ 2 times **more**, YO and draw through all 4 loops on hook.

Base

Rnd 1 (Right side): With Cream, make an adjustable ring and work 6 sc in ring *(Figs. 1a-d, page 46)*; do **not** join, place marker to indicate the beginning of the rnd *(see Markers, page 45)*.

Note: Loop a short piece of yarn around any stitch to mark Rnd 1 as **right** side.

Rnd 2: 2 Sc in each sc around: 12 sc.

Rnd 3: (Sc in next sc, 2 sc in next sc) around: 18 sc.

Rnd 4: (Sc in next 2 sc, 2 sc in next sc) around: 24 sc.

Rnd 5: (Sc in next 3 sc, 2 sc in next sc) around; slip st in next sc, do **not** finish off: 30 sts.

Body

Rnd 6: Ch 1, sc in Back Loop Only of same st as slip st and each sc around *(Fig. 2, page 47)*; join with slip st to **both** loops of first sc: 30 sc.

Rnd 7: Ch 1, sc in same st as joining and in each sc around; join with slip st to first sc.

Rnd 8: Work beginning Cluster in same st as joining, ch 1, skip next sc, ★ work Cluster in next sc, ch 1, skip next sc; repeat from ★ around; join with slip st to top of beginning Cluster: 15 Clusters and 15 chs.

Rnd 9: Ch 1, 2 sc in same st as joining, skip next ch, (2 sc in next Cluster, skip next ch) around; join with a slip st to first sc: 30 sc.

Rnd 10: Ch 1, sc in same st as joining and in each sc around; do **not** join, place marker to indicate the beginning of the rnd.

Rnd 11: Sc in each sc around.

Rnds 12 and 13: Invisible sc2tog, sc in each sc around: 28 sc.

Rnd 14: (Sc in next 5 sc, invisible sc2tog) around: 24 sc.

Rnd 15: Sc in each sc around.

Rnd 16: (Sc in next 4 sc, invisible sc2tog) around: 20 sc.

Rnds 17 and 18: Sc in each sc around.

Rnd 19: (Sc in next 3 sc, invisible sc2tog) around: 16 sc.

Rnd 20: Sc in each sc around.

Stuff Body with polyester fiberfill.

Rnd 21: (Sc in next 2 sc, invisible sc2tog) around: 12 sc.

Rnd 22: (Sc in next sc, invisible sc2tog) around; slip st in next sc and finish off: 8 sts.

Head

Rnd 23: With **right** side facing, join Tan with sc in same st as slip st ***(see Joining With Sc, page 45)***; sc in same st, 2 sc in each sc around; join with slip st to first sc: 16 sc.

Rnd 24: Ch 1, sc in same st as joining and in next 2 sc, 2 sc in next sc, (sc in next 3 sc, 2 sc in next sc) around; do **not** join, place marker to indicate the beginning of the rnd: 20 sc.

Rnds 25-27: Sc in each sc around.

Rnd 28: (Sc in next 3 sc, invisible sc2tog) around: 16 sc.

Stuff Head with polyester fiberfill.

Rnd 29: (Sc in next 2 sc, invisible sc2tog) around: 12 sc.

Rnd 30: (Sc in next sc, invisible sc2tog) around; slip st in next sc and finish off, leaving a 6" (15 cm) end for sewing: 8 sts.

Thread yarn needle with end and weave yarn through Front Loop Only of remaining sc; pull tightly to close and secure end.

Arm (Make 2)

With Cream, leaving a 6" (15 cm) end for sewing and beginning at wrist, ch 7; join with slip st to first ch to form a ring.

Rnd 1 (Right side)**:** Ch 1, 7 sc in ring; do **not** join, place marker to indicate the beginning of the rnd.

Rnds 2-7: Sc in each sc around.

Rnd 8: Invisible sc2tog, sc in next 5 sc: 6 sc.

Rnds 9 and 10: Sc in each sc around; at end of Rnd 10, slip st in next sc and finish off leaving an 8" (20.5 cm) end for sewing.

HAND

Rnd 1 (Right side)**:** With Tan, make an adjustable ring, ch 3, 3 dc in ring; join with slip st to top of beginning ch-3 and finish off.

Thread yarn needle with beginning end of Arm. Insert Hand into beginning ring of Arm and sew in place.

Hair

Rnd 1 (Right side)**:** With Yellow, make an adjustable ring and work 8 sc in ring; do **not** join, place marker to indicate the beginning of the rnd.

Note: Mark Rnd 1 as **right** side.

Rnd 2: 2 Sc in each sc around: 16 sc.

Rnd 3: Sc in each sc around.

Rnd 4: Invisible sc2tog 8 times: 8 sc.

Rnd 5: 2 Sc in each sc around: 16 sc.

Rnd 6: (Sc in next 3 sc, 2 sc in next sc) around: 20 sc.

Rnds 7-11: Sc in each sc around.

Shaping: Slip st in next sc, sc in next sc, hdc in next 2 sc, (hdc, 2 dc) in next sc, skip next sc, slip st in next sc, skip next sc, (2 dc, hdc) in next sc, hdc in next 2 sc, sc in next sc, slip st in next sc and finish off leaving a 10" (25.5 cm) end for sewing.

Cut one 6" (15 cm) strand of Yellow and wrap around base of Rnd 4 to create a bun; tie knot and weave in ends.

Wing (Make 2)

Row 1: With Cream, make an adjustable ring and work 4 sc in ring; do **not** join.

Row 2 (Right side)**:** Ch 1, turn; 2 sc in each sc across: 8 sc.

Note: Mark Row 2 as **right** side.

Row 3: Ch 1, turn; sc in first sc, 2 sc in next sc, (sc in next sc, 2 sc in next sc) across: 12 sc.

Row 4: Ch 1, turn; sc in first 2 sc, 2 sc in next sc, (sc in next 2 sc, 2 sc in next sc) across: 16 sc.

Trim: Ch 1, do **not** turn; work 9 sc evenly spaced across end of rows; ch 3, working in sts on Row 4, slip st in first sc, ch 3, (slip st in next sc, ch 3) across; join with slip st to first sc and finish off leaving a 6" (15 cm) end for sewing.

Block each Wing as follows:
Get each Wing wet with water and then pat with a terry towel to remove excess water.
Pin each Wing to cardboard or blocking mat with straight pins.
Spray evenly with fabric starch if desired; let dry.

Finishing

Using Photos as a guide for placement and using long ends:

- Sew Arms to Body.
- Sew Hair onto Head.
- Sew Wings to back of Body.
- Using Cream, sew cuff of Arms together above the Hands; then tack to Body to hold in place.

Three Wisemen

EASY

SHOPPING LIST

Yarn (Medium Weight) MEDIUM 4

- ☐ Gold - 36 yards (33 meters)
- ☐ Red - 35 yards (32 meters)
- ☐ Rose - 35 yards (32 meters)
- ☐ Dk Blue - 35 yards (32 meters)
- ☐ Tan - 18 yards (16.5 meters)
- ☐ Grey - 18 yards (16.5 meters)
- ☐ Brown - 9 yards (8.25 meters)

Crochet Hook

- ☐ Size D (3.25 mm) **or** size needed for gauge

Additional Supplies

- ☐ Yarn needle
- ☐ Polyester fiberfill

STITCH GUIDE

INVISIBLE SINGLE CROCHET 2 TOGETHER *(abbreviated invisible sc2tog)*

Pull up a loop in Front Loop Only of each of next 2 sts *(Fig. 2, page 47)*, YO and draw through all 3 loops on hook **(counts as one sc)**.

WISEMAN #1

Finished Size: 5¾" (14.5 cm) tall

Gauge Information

Gauge Swatch: 2" (5 cm) diameter

Work same as Base: 30 sts.

Base

Rnd 1 (Right side): With Red, make an adjustable ring and work 6 sc in ring ***(Figs. 1a-d, page 46)***; do **not** join, place marker to indicate the beginning of the rnd ***(see Markers, page 45)***.

Note: Loop a short piece of yarn around any stitch to mark Rnd 1 as **right** side.

Rnd 2: 2 Sc in each sc around: 12 sc.

Rnd 3: (Sc in next sc, 2 sc in next sc) around: 18 sc.

Rnd 4: (Sc in next 2 sc, 2 sc in next sc) around: 24 sc.

Rnd 5: (Sc in next 3 sc, 2 sc in next sc) around; slip st in next sc, do **not** finish off: 30 sts.

Body

Rnd 6: Ch 1, sc in Back Loop Only of same st as slip st and each sc around ***(Fig. 2, page 47)***; join with slip st to **both** loops of first sc: 30 sc.

Rnd 7: Ch 1, sc in same st as joining and in each sc around; join with slip st to first sc changing to Gold ***(Fig. 4a, page 47)***, drop Red to **wrong** side of work.

Rnd 8: With Gold ch 1, sc in same st as joining and in each sc around; join with slip st to first sc changing to Red; drop Gold to **wrong** side of work.

Rnd 9: With Red ch 1, sc in same st as joining and in each sc around; join with a slip st to first sc.

Drop unused color to **wrong** side of work; do **not** cut unused color until indicated.

Rnd 10: Ch 1, sc in same st as joining changing to Gold ***(Fig. 4b, page 47)***, sc in next sc changing to Red, ★ sc in next sc changing to Gold, sc in next sc changing to Red; repeat from ★ around to last sc, sc in last sc; join with slip st to first sc.

Rnd 11: With Red ch 1, sc in same st as joining and in each sc around; join with slip st to first sc changing to Gold.

Rnd 12: With Gold ch 1, sc in same st as joining and in each sc around; join with slip st to first sc changing to Red, cut Gold.

Rnd 13: With Red ch 1, sc in same st as joining and in each sc around; do **not** join, place marker to indicate the beginning of the rnd.

Rnd 14: Sc in each sc around.

Rnds 15 and 16: Invisible sc2tog, sc in each sc around: 28 sc.

Rnd 17: (Sc in next 5 sc, invisible sc2tog) around: 24 sc.

Rnds 18 and 19: Sc in each sc around.

Rnd 20: (Sc in next 4 sc, invisible sc2tog) around: 20 sc.

Rnds 21 and 22: Sc in each sc around.

Rnd 23: (Sc in next 3 sc, invisible sc2tog) around: 16 sc.

Rnd 24: Sc in each sc around.

Stuff Body with polyester fiberfill.

Rnd 25: (Sc in next 2 sc, invisible sc2tog) around: 12 sc.

Rnd 26: (Sc in next sc, invisible sc2tog) around; slip st in next sc and finish off: 8 sts.

Head

Rnd 27: With **right** side facing, join Tan with sc in same st as slip st ***(see Joining With Sc, page 45)***; sc in same st, 2 sc in each sc around; join with slip st to first sc: 16 sc.

Rnd 28: Ch 1, sc in same st as joining and in next 2 sc, 2 sc in next sc, (sc in next 3 sc, 2 sc in next sc) around; do **not** join, place marker to indicate the beginning of the rnd: 20 sc.

Rnds 29-31: Sc in each sc around.

Rnd 32: (Sc in next 3 sc, invisible sc2tog) around: 16 sc.

Stuff Head with polyester fiberfill.

Rnd 33: (Sc in next 2 sc, invisible sc2tog) around: 12 sc.

Rnd 34: (Sc in next sc, invisible sc2tog) around; slip st in next sc and finish off leaving a 6" (15 cm) end for sewing: 8 sts.

Thread yarn needle with end and weave yarn through Front Loop Only of remaining sc; pull tightly to close and secure end.

Arm (Make 2)

With Red, leaving a 6" (15 cm) end for sewing and beginning at wrist, ch 7; join with slip st to first ch to form a ring.

Rnd 1 (Right side): Ch 1, 7 sc in ring; do **not** join, place marker to indicate the beginning of the rnd.

Note: Mark Rnd 1 as **right** side.

Rnds 2-7: Sc in each sc around.

Rnd 8: Invisible sc2tog, sc in next 5 sc: 6 sc.

Rnds 9-11: Sc in each sc around; at end of Rnd 11, slip st in next sc and finish off leaving an 8" (20.5 cm) end for sewing.

HAND

Rnd 1 (Right side): With Tan, make an adjustable ring, ch 3, 3 dc in ring; join with slip st to top of beginning ch-3 and finish off.

Thread yarn needle with beginning end of Arm. Insert Hand into beginning ring of Arm and sew in place.

Headdress

Rnd 1 (Right side): With Red, make an adjustable ring and work 6 sc in ring; do **not** join, place marker to indicate the beginning of the rnd.

Note: Mark Rnd 1 as **right** side.

Rnd 2: 2 Sc in each sc around: 12 sc.

Rnd 3: (Sc in next sc, 2 sc in next sc) around: 18 sc.

Rnd 4: (Sc in next 8 sc, 2 sc in next sc) twice; slip st in next sc changing to Gold; drop Red to **wrong** side of work: 20 sc.

Rnd 5: With Gold ch 1, sc in same st as slip st and in each sc around; join with slip st to first sc changing to Red; cut Gold.

Rnd 6: With Red ch 1, sc in same st as joining and in each sc around; join with slip st to first sc, do **not** finish off.

FLAP

Row 1 (Right side): Ch 1, sc in same st as joining and in next 13 sc, leave remaining 6 sc unworked: 14 sc.

Rows 2-8: Ch 1, turn, sc in each sc across.

Finish off.

Row 9: With **right** side facing, join Gold with sc in first sc; sc in each sc across; finish off.

Beard

Row 1: With Brown and leaving a 6" (15 cm) end for sewing, ch 5; sc in second ch from hook and in each ch across: 4 sc.

Row 2: Ch 1, turn; sc in each sc across.

Row 3: Ch 1, turn; beginning in first sc, sc2tog twice: 2 sc.

Row 4: Ch 1, turn; beginning in first sc, sc2tog; finish off: one sc.

Finishing

Using Photo as a guide for placement and using long ends:

- Sew Arms to Body.
- With Red, sew Headdress to Head.
- Sew Beard to Head.
- Using Red, sew cuff of Arms together above the Hands; then tack to Body to hold in place.

#3
#2
#1

WISEMAN #2

Finished Size: 5¾" (14.5 cm) tall

Gauge Information

Gauge Swatch: 2" (5 cm) diameter
Work same as Base: 30 sts.

Base

Rnd 1 (Right side): With Gold, make an adjustable ring and work 6 sc in ring ***(Figs. 1a-d, page 46)***; do **not** join, place marker to indicate the beginning of the rnd ***(see Markers, page 45)***.

Note: Loop a short piece of yarn around any stitch to mark Rnd 1 as **right** side.

Rnd 2: 2 Sc in each sc around: 12 sc.

Rnd 3: (Sc in next sc, 2 sc in next sc) around: 18 sc.

Rnd 4: (Sc in next 2 sc, 2 sc in next sc) around: 24 sc.

Rnd 5: (Sc in next 3 sc, 2 sc in next sc) around; slip st in next sc, do **not** finish off: 30 sts.

Body

Rnd 6: Ch 1, sc in Back Loop Only of same st as slip st and each sc around ***(Fig. 2, page 47)***; join with slip st to **both** loops of first sc: 30 sc.

Rnd 7: Ch 1, sc in same st as joining and in each sc around; do **not** join, place marker to indicate the beginning of the rnd.

Rnds 8 and 9: Sc in each sc around; at end of Rnd 9, slip st in next sc and finish off.

Rnd 10: With **right** side facing, join Rose with sc in same st as slip st ***(see Joining With Sc, page 45)***; sc in each sc around; join with slip st to first sc.

Rnd 11: Ch 1, sc in same st as joining and in each sc around; do **not** join, place marker to indicate the beginning of the rnd.

Rnds 12-14: Sc in each sc around.

Rnds 15 and 16: Invisible sc2tog, sc in each sc around: 28 sc.

Rnd 17: (Sc in next 5 sc, invisible sc2tog) around: 24 sc.

Rnds 18 and 19: Sc in each sc around.

Rnd 20: (Sc in next 4 sc, invisible sc2tog) around: 20 sc.

Rnds 21 and 22: Sc in each sc around.

Rnd 23: (Sc in next 3 sc, invisible sc2tog) around: 16 sc.

Rnd 24: Sc in each sc around.

Stuff Body with polyester fiberfill.

Rnd 25: (Sc in next 2 sc, invisible sc2tog) around: 12 sc.

Rnd 26: (Sc in next sc, invisible sc2tog) around; slip st in next sc and finish off: 8 sts.

Head

Rnd 27: With **right** side facing, join Tan with sc in same st as slip st; sc in same st, 2 sc in each sc around; join with slip st to first sc: 16 sc.

Rnd 28: Ch 1, sc in same st as joining and in next 2 sc, 2 sc in next sc, (sc in next 3 sc, 2 sc in next sc) around; do **not** join, place marker to indicate the beginning of the rnd: 20 sc.

Rnds 29-31: Sc in each sc around.

Rnd 32: (Sc in next 3 sc, invisible sc2tog) around: 16 sc.

Stuff Head with polyester fiberfill.

Rnd 33: (Sc in next 2 sc, invisible sc2tog) around: 12 sc.

Rnd 34: (Sc in next sc, invisible sc2tog) around; slip st in next sc and finish off leaving a 6" (15 cm) end for sewing: 8 sts.

Thread yarn needle with end and weave yarn through Front Loop Only of remaining sc; pull tightly to close and secure end.

Arm (Make 2)

With Rose, leaving a 6" (15 cm) end for sewing and beginning at wrist, ch 7; join with slip st to first ch to form a ring.

Rnd 1 (Right side): Ch 1, 7 sc in ring; do **not** join, place marker to indicate the beginning of the rnd.

Note: Mark Rnd 1 as **right** side.

Rnds 2-7: Sc in each sc around.

Rnd 8: Invisible sc2tog, sc in next 5 sc: 6 sc.

Rnds 9-11: Sc in each sc around; at end of Rnd 11, slip st in next sc and finish off leaving an 8" (20.5 cm) end for sewing.

HAND

Rnd 1 (Right side): With Tan, make an adjustable ring, ch 3, 3 dc in ring; join with slip st to top of beginning ch-3 and finish off.

Thread yarn needle with beginning end of Arm. Insert Hand into beginning ring of Arm and sew in place.

Headdress

Rnd 1 (Right side): With Rose, make an adjustable ring and work 6 sc in ring; do **not** join, place marker to indicate the beginning of the rnd.

Note: Mark Rnd 1 as **right** side.

Rnd 2: 2 Sc in each sc around: 12 sc.

Rnd 3: (Sc in next sc, 2 sc in next sc) around: 18 sc.

Rnd 4: (Sc in next 8 sc, 2 sc in next sc) twice; slip st in next sc changing to Gold ***(Fig. 4a, page 47)***; drop Rose to **wrong** side of work: 20 sc.

Rnd 5: With Gold ch 1, sc in same st as slip st and in each sc around; join with slip st to first sc changing to Rose; cut Gold.

Rnd 6: With Rose ch 1, sc in same st as joining and in each sc around; join with slip st to first sc, do **not** finish off.

FLAP

Row 1 (Right side): Ch 1, sc in same st as joining and in next 13 sc, leave remaining 6 sc unworked: 14 sc.

Rows 2-8: Ch 1, turn; sc in each sc across.

Finish off.

Row 9: With **right** side facing, join Gold with sc in first sc; sc in each sc across; finish off.

Beard

With Brown, ch 7; join with slip st to first ch to form a ring.

Rnd 1 (Right side): Ch 1, (sc, 2 dc, sc) in ring, finish off leaving half of ch-ring unworked.

Scarf

Row 1 (Right side): With Lt Grey, ch 35; hdc in second ch from hook and in each ch across; finish off.

Finishing

Using Photo as a guide for placement and using long ends:

- Sew Arms to Body.
- With Rose, sew Headdress to Head.
- Sew Beard to Head.
- Using Rose, sew cuff of Arms together above the Hands; then tack to Body to hold in place.
- Wrap Scarf around neck and tuck each end under arms to hold in place.

WISEMAN #3

Finished Size: 5¾" (14.5 cm) tall

Gauge Information

Gauge Swatch: 2" (5 cm) diameter

Work same as Base: 30 sts.

Base

Rnd 1 (Right side): With Lt Grey, make an adjustable ring and work 6 sc in ring ***(Figs. 1a-d, page 46)***; do **not** join, place marker to indicate the beginning of the rnd ***(see Markers, page 45)***.

Note: Loop a short piece of yarn around any stitch to mark Rnd 1 as **right** side.

Rnd 2: 2 Sc in each sc around: 12 sc.

Rnd 3: (Sc in next sc, 2 sc in next sc) around: 18 sc.

Rnd 4: (Sc in next 2 sc, 2 sc in next sc) around: 24 sc.

Rnd 5: (Sc in next 3 sc, 2 sc in next sc) around; slip st in next sc, do **not** finish off: 30 sts.

Body

Rnd 6: Ch 1, sc in Back Loop Only of same st as slip st and each sc around ***(Fig. 2, page 47)***; join with slip st to **both** loops of first sc, finish off: 30 sc.

Rnd 7: With **right** side facing, join Dk Blue with sc in same sc as joining ***(see Joining With Sc, page 45)***; sc in each sc around; join with slip st to first sc changing to Gold ***(Fig. 4a, page 47)***, drop Dk Blue to **wrong** side of work.

Rnd 8: With Gold ch 1, sc in same st as joining and in each sc around; join with slip st to first sc changing to Dk Blue; drop Gold to **wrong** side of work.

Rnd 9: With Dk Blue ch 1, sc in same st as joining and in each sc around; join with slip st to first sc.

Rnd 10: Ch 1, sc in same st as joining and in each sc around; join with slip st to first sc changing to Gold; drop Dk Blue to **wrong** side of work.

Drop unused color to **wrong** side of work; do **not** cut unused color until indicated.

Rnd 11: With Gold ch 1, sc in same st as joining changing to Lt Grey ***(Fig. 4b, page 47)***, (sc in next sc changing to Gold, sc in next sc changing to Lt Grey) around to last sc, sc in last sc, cut Lt Grey; join with slip st to first sc changing to Dk Blue.

Rnd 12: With Dk Blue ch 1, sc in same st as joining and in each sc around; join with slip st to first sc.

Rnd 13: Ch 1, sc in same st as joining and in each sc around; join with slip st to first sc changing to Gold.

Rnd 14: With Gold ch 1, sc in same st as joining and in each sc around; join with slip st to first sc changing to Dk Blue; cut Gold.

Rnd 15: With Dk Blue ch 1, sc in same st as joining and in each sc around; join with slip st to first sc changing to Lt Grey.

Rnd 16: With Lt Grey ch 1, sc in same st as joining and in each sc around; join with slip st to first sc changing to Dk Blue; cut Lt Grey.

Rnd 17: Ch 1, beginning in same st as joining, (invisible sc2tog, sc in next 13 sc) twice; do **not** join, place marker to indicate the beginning of the rnd: 28 sc.

Rnd 18: (Sc in next 5 sc, invisible sc2tog) around: 24 sc.

Rnd 19: Sc in each sc around.

Rnd 20: (Sc in next 4 sc, invisible sc2tog) around: 20 sc.

Rnds 21 and 22: Sc in each sc around.

Rnd 23: (Sc in next 3 sc, invisible sc2tog) around: 16 sc.

Rnd 24: Sc in each sc around.

Stuff Body with polyester fiberfill.

Rnd 25: (Sc in next 2 sc, invisible sc2tog) around: 12 sc.

Rnd 26: (Sc in next sc, invisible sc2tog) around; slip st in next sc and finish off: 8 sts.

Head

Rnd 27: With **right** side facing, join Tan with sc in same st as slip st; sc in same st, 2 sc in each sc around; join with slip st to first sc: 16 sc.

Rnd 28: Ch 1, sc in same st as joining and in next 2 sc, 2 sc in next sc, (sc in next 3 sc, 2 sc in next sc) around; do **not** join, place marker to indicate the beginning of the rnd: 20 sc.

Rnds 29-31: Sc in each sc around.

Rnd 32: (Sc in next 3 sc, invisible sc2tog) around: 16 sc.

Stuff Head with polyester fiberfill.

Rnd 33: (Sc in next 2 sc, invisible sc2tog) around: 12 sc.

Rnd 34: (Sc in next sc, invisible sc2tog) around; slip st in next sc and finish off leaving a 6" (15 cm) end for sewing: 8 sts.

Thread yarn needle with end and weave yarn through Front Loop Only of remaining sc; pull tightly to close and secure end.

Arm (Make 2)

With Dk Blue, leaving a 6" (15 cm) end for sewing and beginning at wrist, ch 7; join with slip st to first ch to form a ring.

Rnd 1 (Right side): Ch 1, 7 sc in ring; do **not** join, place marker to indicate the beginning of the rnd.

Note: Mark Rnd 1 as **right** side.

Rnds 2-7: Sc in each sc around.

Rnd 8: Invisible sc2tog, sc in next 5 sc: 6 sc.

Rnds 9-11: Sc in each sc around; at end of Rnd 11, slip st in next sc and finish off leaving an 8" (20.5 cm) end for sewing.

HAND

Rnd 1 (Right side): With Tan, make an adjustable ring, ch 3, 3 dc in ring; join with slip st to top of beginning ch-3 and finish off.

Thread yarn needle with beginning end of Arm. Insert Hand into beginning ring of Arm and sew in place.

Headdress

Rnd 1 (Right side): With Dk Blue, make an adjustable ring and work 6 sc in ring; do **not** join, place marker to indicate the beginning of the rnd.

Note: Mark Rnd 1 as **right** side.

Rnd 2: 2 Sc in each sc around: 12 sc.

Rnd 3: (Sc in next sc, 2 sc in next sc) around: 18 sc.

Rnd 4: (Sc in next 8 sc, 2 sc in next sc) twice: 20 sc.

Rnds 5 and 6: Sc in each sc around; do **not** finish off.

FLAP

Row 1 (Wrong side): Ch 1, **turn**; sc in first 14 sc, leave remaining 6 sc unworked.

Rows 2-7: Ch 1, turn; sc in each sc across.

Finish off.

Row 8: With **right** side facing, join Gold with sc in first sc; sc in each sc across; finish off.

Beard

Row 1 (Right side): With Brown, ch 9; sc in second ch from hook, hdc in next ch, 2 hdc in next ch, skip next 2 chs, 2 hdc in next ch, hdc in next ch, sc in last ch; finish off leaving an 8" (20.5 cm) end for sewing.

Finishing

Using Photo as a guide for placement and using long ends:

- Sew Arms to Body.
- With Dk Blue, sew Headdress to Head.
- Sew Beard to Head.
- Using Dk Blue, sew cuff of Arms together above the Hands; then tack to Body to hold in place.

Camel

EASY

Finished Size: 3¼" tall x 5¼" wide (8.25 cm x 13.25 cm)

SHOPPING LIST

Yarn (Medium Weight) MEDIUM 4

- ☐ Lt Brown - 39 yards (35.5 meters)
- ☐ Red - 10 yards (9 meters)
- ☐ Brown - 8 yards (7.5 meters)
- ☐ Yellow - 6 yards (5.5 meters)

Crochet Hook

- ☐ Size D (3.25 mm) **or** size needed for gauge

Additional Supplies

- ☐ Yarn needle
- ☐ Polyester fiberfill

STITCH GUIDE

INVISIBLE SINGLE CROCHET 2 TOGETHER
(abbreviated invisible sc2tog)
Pull up a loop in Front Loop Only of each of next 2 sts ***(Fig. 2, page 47)***, YO and draw through all 3 loops on hook **(counts as one sc)**.

Gauge Information

22 sc and 20 rows/rounds = 4" (10 cm)

Gauge Swatch: 4" (10 cm) square

Ch 23.

Row 1: Sc in second ch from hook and in each ch across: 22 sc.

Rows 2-20: Ch 1, turn; sc in each sc across.

Finish off.

Body

Rnd 1 (Right side): With Lt Brown, make an adjustable ring and work 6 sc in ring ***(Figs. 1a-d, page 46)***; do **not** join, place marker to indicate the beginning of the rnd ***(see Markers, page 45)***.

Note: Loop a short piece of yarn around any stitch to mark Rnd 1 as **right** side.

Rnd 2: 2 Sc in each sc around: 12 sc.

Rnds 3 and 4: Sc in each sc around.

Rnd 5: (Sc in next sc, 2 sc in next sc) around: 18 sc.

Rnd 6: Sc in each sc around.

Rnd 7: (Sc in next 2 sc, 2 sc in next sc) around: 24 sc.

Rnd 8: (Sc in next 3 sc, 2 sc in next sc) around: 30 sc.

Rnd 9: Sc in each sc around.

Rnd 10: (Sc in next 2 sc, 2 sc in next sc) around: 40 sc.

Rnds 11-16: Sc in each sc around.

Rnd 17: ★ Sc in next 12 sc, invisible sc2tog 4 times; repeat from ★ once **more**: 32 sc.

Rnd 18: Sc in each sc around.

Rnd 19: ★ Sc in next 8 sc, invisible sc2tog 4 times; repeat from ★ once more: 24 sc.

Rnd 20: ★ Sc in next 4 sc, invisible sc2tog 4 times; repeat from ★ once **more**; slip st in next sc and finish off leaving an 8" (20.5 cm) end for sewing: 16 sts.

Stuff Body with polyester fiberfill.

Thread yarn needle with end and sew opening closed.

Head & Neck

Rnd 1 (Right side): With Lt Brown, make an adjustable ring and work 6 sc in ring; do **not** join, place marker to indicate the beginning of the rnd.

Note: Mark Rnd 1 as **right** side.

Rnd 2: 2 Sc in each sc around: 12 sc.

Rnd 3: (Sc in next 2 sc, 2 sc in next sc) around: 16 sc.

Rnds 4-7: Sc in each sc around.

Rnd 8: (Sc in next 6 sc, invisible sc2tog) twice: 14 sc.

Rnds 9-12: Sc in each sc around.

Rnd 13: Slip st in next 9 sc, hdc in next 5 sc.

Rnds 14 and 15: Sc in each st around.

Rnd 16: (Sc in next sc, 2 sc in next sc) 5 times, hdc in next 4 sc: 19 sts.

Rnds 17 and 18: Sc in each st around; at end of Rnd 18, slip st in next sc and finish off leaving an 8" (20.5 cm) end for sewing.

Stuff Head and Neck with polyester fiberfill.

SNOUT

Rnd 1 (Right side): With Lt Brown, make an adjustable ring and work 4 sc in ring; do **not** join, place marker to indicate the beginning of the rnd.

Note: Mark Rnd 1 as **right** side.

Rnd 2: 2 Sc in each sc around: 8 sc.

Rnds 3-5: Sc in each sc around; at end of Rnd 5, slip st in next sc and finish off leaving a 6" (15 cm) end for sewing.

Ear (Make 2)

Rnd 1 (Right side): With Lt Brown, make an adjustable ring and work 5 sc in ring; do **not** join, place marker to indicate the beginning of the rnd.

Note: Mark Rnd 1 as **right** side.

Rnd 2: Sc in each sc around; slip st in next sc and finish off leaving a 6" (15 cm) end for sewing.

Leg (Make 4)

Rnd 1 (Right side): With Brown, make an adjustable ring and work 4 sc in ring; do **not** join, place marker to indicate the beginning of the rnd.

Note: Mark Rnd 1 as **right** side.

Rnd 2: (Sc in next sc, 2 sc in next sc) twice: 6 sc.

Rnd 3: Sc in each sc around; slip st in next sc and finish off.

Rnd 4: With **right** side facing, join Lt Brown with sc in same st as slip st ***(see Joining With Sc, page 45)***; sc in each sc around; join with slip st to first sc: 6 sc.

Rnd 5: Ch 1, sc in same st as joining and in each sc around, do **not** join; place marker to indicate the beginning of the rnd.

Rnds 6-18: Sc in each sc around; at end of Rnd 18, slip st in next sc and finish off leaving an 8" (10.5 cm) end for sewing.

Blanket

Rnd 1 (Right side): With Red, make an adjustable ring and work 6 sc in ring; do **not** join, place marker to indicate the beginning of the rnd.

Note: Mark Rnd 1 as **right** side.

Rnd 2: 2 Sc in each sc around: 12 sc.

Rnds 3 and 4: Sc in each sc around.

Rnd 5: (Sc in next sc, 2 sc in next sc) around: 18 sc.

Rnd 6: Sc in each sc around.

Rnds 7 and 8: (Sc in next 2 sc, 2 sc in next sc) around: 32 sc.

Rnd 9: ★ Sc in next 7 sc, (sc, ch 2, sc) in next sc; repeat from ★ around; slip st in next sc and finish off: 36 sc and 4 ch-2 sps.

Rnd 10: With **right** side facing, join Yellow with sc in any ch-2 sp; ch 2, sc in same sp and in next 9 sc, ★(sc, ch 2, sc) in next ch-2 sp, sc in next 9 sc; repeat from ★ 2 times **more**; join with slip st to first sc, finish off: 44 sc and 4 ch-2 sps.

Rnd 11: With **right** side facing, join Red with sc in any ch-2 sp; ch 2, sc in same sp and in next 11 sc, ★ (sc, ch 2, sc) in next ch-2 sp, sc in next 11 sc; repeat from ★ 2 times **more**; join with slip st to first sc, finish off: 52 sc and 4 ch-2 sps.

FRINGE

Cut twelve, 3" (7.5 cm) strands of Yellow.

Holding 3 strands together, fold in half. Insert crochet hook in ch-2 sp from the **wrong** side. Pull folded end of strands through and draw loose ends though folded end. Pull ends to tighten.

Repeat on remaining 3 ch-2 sps.

Trim ends evenly.

Rope

With Brown, ch 18; being careful **not** to twist ch, join with slip st to first ch to form a ring; ch 28, skip next 8 chs, slip st in next ch; finish off.

Finishing

Using Photos as a guide for placement and using long ends:

- Sew Snout and Ears to Head.
- Sew Neck to Body.
- Pull Head back toward Body and tack neck in place with Lt Brown.
- For 2 front Legs, fold Leg in half and using photo as a guide, sew on Body. Sew first half flat to body then pull the other half up and secure.
- Sew back Legs in same manner, folding them in the opposite direction.
- With Red, sew Blanket in place over hump.
- Place ropes over head and stitch in place to secure.

GENERAL INSTRUCTIONS

Abbreviations

ch(s)	chain(s)
cm	centimeters
dc	double crochet(s)
hdc	half double crochet(s)
mm	millimeters
Rnd(s)	Round(s)
sc	single crochet(s)
sc2tog	single crochet 2 together
sp(s)	space(s)
st(s)	stitch(es)
YO	yarn over

Symbols & Terms

★ — work instructions following ★ as many **more** times as indicated in addition to the first time.

( ) or **[ ]** — work enclosed instructions **as many** times as specified by the number immediately following **or** work all enclosed instructions in the stitch or space indicated **or** contains explanatory remarks.

colon (:) — the number(s) given after a colon at the end of a row or round denote(s) the number of stitches you should have on that row or round.

CROCHET TERMINOLOGY		
UNITED STATES		INTERNATIONAL
slip stitch (slip st)	=	single crochet (sc)
single crochet (sc)	=	double crochet (dc)
half double crochet (hdc)	=	half treble crochet (htr)
double crochet (dc)	=	treble crochet (tr)
treble crochet (tr)	=	double treble crochet (dtr)
double treble crochet (dtr)	=	triple treble crochet (ttr)
triple treble crochet (tr tr)	=	quadruple treble crochet (qtr)
skip	=	miss

BASIC	Projects using basic stitches. May include basic increases and decreases.
EASY	Projects may include simple stitch patterns, color work, and/or shaping.
INTERMEDIATE	Projects may include involved stitch patterns, color work, and/or shaping.
COMPLEX	Projects may include complex stitch patterns, color work, and/or shaping using a variety of techniques and stitches simultaneously.

CROCHET HOOKS																	
U.S.	B-1	C-2	D-3	E-4	F-5	G-6	7	H-8	I-9	J-10	K-10½	L-11	M/N-13	N/P-15	P/Q	Q	S
Metric - mm	2.25	2.75	3.25	3.5	3.75	4	4.5	5	5.5	6	6.5	8	9	10	15	16	19

Gauge

Exact gauge is **essential** for proper size. Before beginning your project, make the sample swatch given in the instructions in the yarn and hook specified. After completing the swatch, measure it, counting your stitches and rows or rounds carefully. If your swatch is larger or smaller than specified, **make another, changing hook size to get the correct gauge**. Keep trying until you find the size hook that will give you the specified gauge.

Markers

Markers are used to help distinguish the beginning of each round being worked. Place a 2" (5 cm) scrap piece of yarn before the first stitch of each round, moving marker after each round is complete.

Joining With Sc

When instructed to join with sc, begin with a slip knot on the hook. Insert hook in stitch indicated, YO and pull up a loop, YO and draw through both loops on hook.

Yarn Weight Symbol & Names	LACE 0	SUPER FINE 1	FINE 2	LIGHT 3	MEDIUM 4	BULKY 5	SUPER BULKY 6	JUMBO 7
Type of Yarns in Category	Fingering, size 10 crochet thread	Sock, Fingering, Baby	Sport, Baby	DK, Light Worsted	Worsted, Afghan, Aran	Chunky, Craft, Rug	Super Bulky, Roving	Jumbo, Roving
Crochet Gauge* Ranges in Single Crochet to 4" (10 cm)	32-42 sts**	21-32 sts	16-20 sts	12-17 sts	11-14 sts	8-11 sts	6-9 sts	5 sts and fewer
Advised Hook Size Range	Steel*** 6 to 8, Regular hook B-1	B-1 to E-4	E-4 to 7	7 to I-9	I-9 to K-10½	K-10½ to M/N-13	M/N-13 to Q	Q and larger

*GUIDELINES ONLY: The chart above reflects the most commonly used gauges and hook sizes for specific yarn categories.

** Lace weight yarns are usually crocheted with larger hooks to create lacy openwork patterns. Accordingly, a gauge range is difficult to determine. Always follow the gauge stated in your pattern.

*** Steel crochet hooks are sized differently from regular hooks–the higher the number, the smaller the hook, which is the reverse of regular hook sizing.

Adjustable Loop

Wind the yarn around two fingers to form a ring ***(Fig. 1a)***, slide the yarn off your fingers and grasp the strands at the top of the ring ***(Fig. 1b)***. Insert the hook from **front** to **back** into the ring, pull up a loop, YO and draw through the loop on hook to lock the ring ***(Fig. 1c)***. Working around **both** strands, work stitches in the ring as specified, then pull the yarn end to close ***(Fig. 1d)***.

Fig. 1a

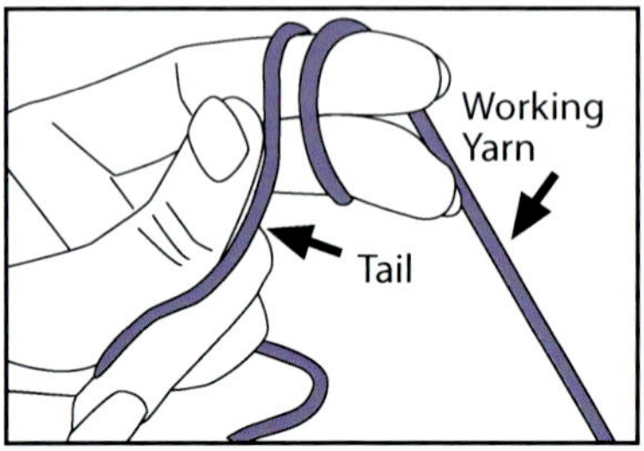

Fig. 1b

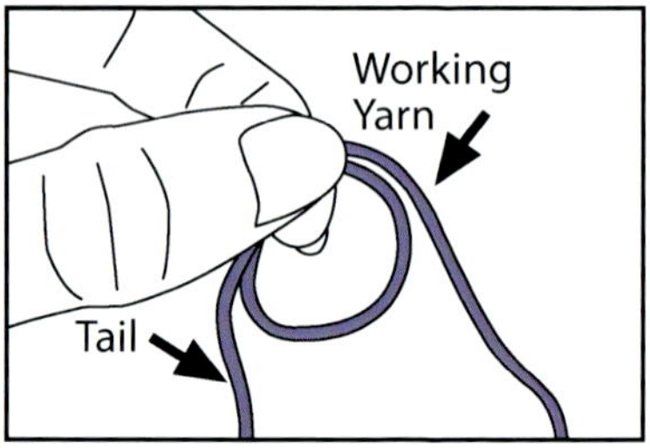

Fig. 1c

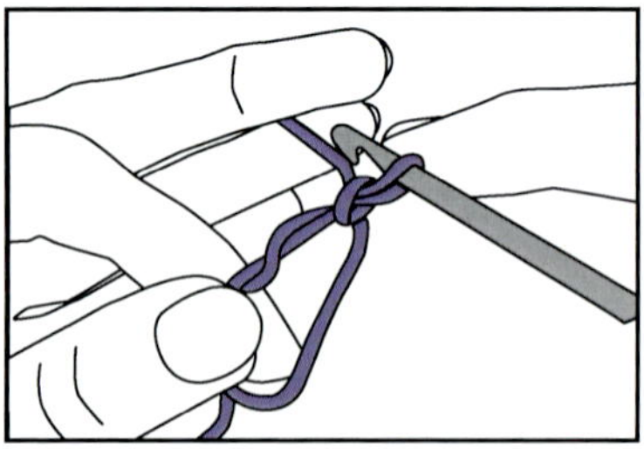

Fig. 1d

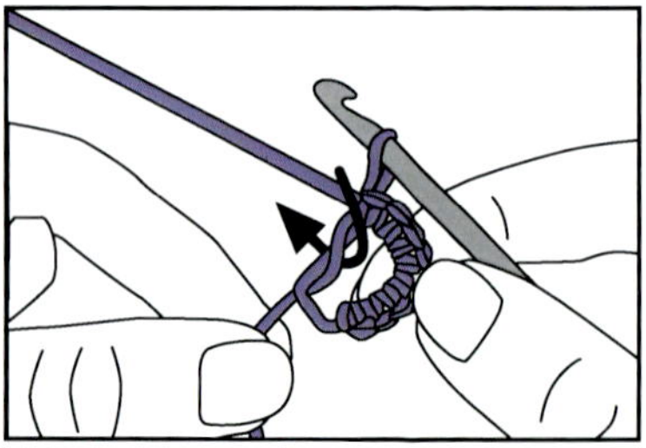

Back Or Front Loops Only

Work only in loop(s) indicated by arrow *(Fig. 2)*.

Fig. 2

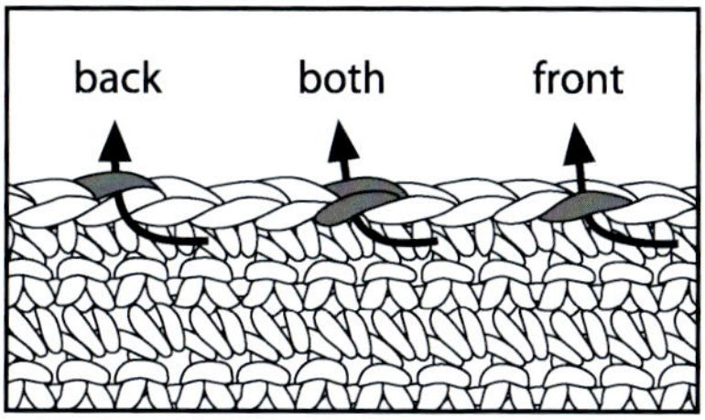

Free Loop

After working in Back of Front Loops Only on a row or round, there will be a ridge of unused loops. These are called the free loops. Later, when instructed to work in the free loops of the same row or round, work in these loops *(Fig. 3)*.

Fig. 3

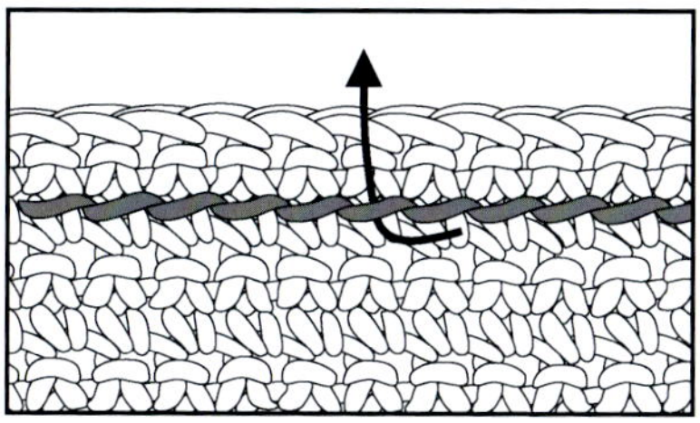

Changing Colors

Work the last stitch to within one step of completion hook new yarn (***Figs. 4a & 4b)*** and draw through all loops on hook. Do **not** cut old color unless otherwise indicated.

Fig. 4a

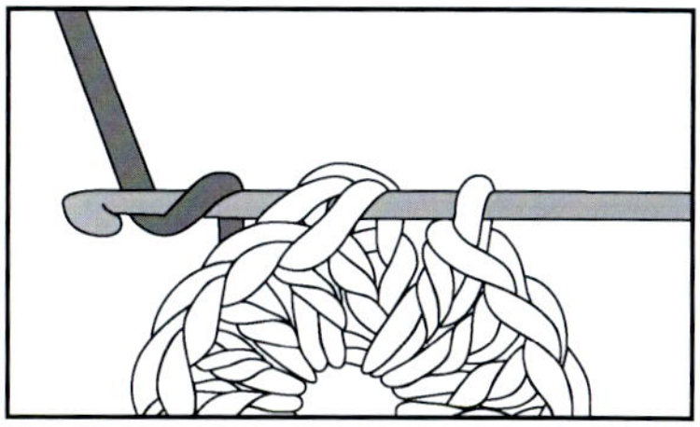

Fig. 4b

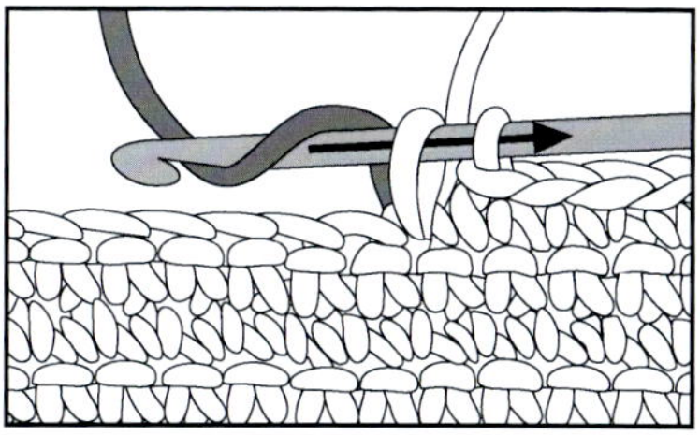

YARN INFORMATION

The projects in this book were made using Medium Weight Yarn. Any brand of medium weight yarn may be used. It is best to refer to the yardage/meters when determining how many balls or skeins to purchase. Remember, to arrive at the finished size, it is the GAUGE/TENSION that is important, not the brand of yarn.

For your convenience, listed below are the specific yarns used to create our photography models. Because yarn manufacturers make frequent changes to their product lines, you may sometimes find it necessary to use a substitute yarn or to search for the discontinued product at alternate suppliers (locally or online).

HOLY FAMILY

Lion Brand® Basic Stitch® Anti-Pilling
Brown - #126 Mahogany
Cream - #099 Ivory
Lt Blue - #106 Baby Blue
Tan - #121 Almond
Lt Brown - #134 Honey
Dk Blue - #109 Steel Blue
Red Heart® Chic Sheep by Marly Bird™
Yellow - #5324 Mimosa

ANGEL

Lion Brand® Basic Stitch® Anti-Pilling
Cream - #099 Ivory
Tan - #121 Almond
Red Heart® Chic Sheep by Marly Bird™
Yellow - #5324 Mimosa

THREE WISEMEN

Lion Brand® Basic Stitch® Anti-Pilling
Gold - #134 Honey
Red - #400 Red Heather
Dk Blue - #109 Steel Blue
Tan - #121 Almond
Brown - #126 Mahogany
Red Heart® Chic Sheep by Marly Bird™
Rose - #5628 Vineyard
Grey - #5640 Platinum

CAMEL

Lion Brand® Basic Stitch® Anti-Pilling
Lt Brown - #123 Cedarwood
Red - #400 Red Heather
Brown - #126 Mahogany
Red Heart® Chic Sheep by Marly Bird™
Yellow - #5324 Mimosa

Made in U.S.A.